Books by Edward Dorn

Poetry

The Newly Fallen
Hands Up!
Geography
Idaho Out
North Atlantic Turbine
Twenty-Four Love Songs
Songs Set Two—A Short Count
Recollections of Gran Apacheria
Collected Poems
Manchester Square (with Jennifer Dorn)
Gunslinger

Prose

The Rites of Passage
(Revised later as By the Sound)
Some Business Recently Transacted in the White World

Nonfiction

The Shoshoneans
(with photographs by Leroy Lucas)

Translation

(with Gordon Brotherston)

The Tree Between Two Walls
Our Word
Cesar Vallejo Selected Poems

Screenplay

Abilene! Abilene!

HELLO, LA JOLLA

Edward Dorn

Wingbow Press 1978 Berkeley

Wingbow Press books are published and distributed by Bookpeople, 2940 Seventh Street, Berkeley, California 94710

Cover Art by Michael Patrick Cronan
Backcover photograph by Lynne Domash
Interior photograph by Jennifer Dorn

ISBN 0-914728-23-2 Trade Paper Edition
ISBN 0-914728-24-0 Trade Cloth Edition
ISBN 0-914728-25-3 Signed Cloth Edition

Library of Congress Catalog Card Number 78-50780

First Edition June 1978

Contents

AMONG THE DRAPERIES OF DEFINITION

1 0 1

PREFACE

These dispatches should be
received in the spirit
of the Pony Express:
light and essential.

A for Ism

A poets occupation
is to compose poetry
The writing of it
is everywhere

"In lands like Southern California, where flowers fill the air with fragrance, where fruits are so abundant that starvation is impossible, and where the nerves are not continually whipped by atmospheric changes into restless energy, men live more calmly, probably more rationally."

—JOHN L. STODDARD, 1898

HELLO LA JOLLA

Suppertime Down South

The ceaseless jets of Miramar
Make their planar way to the Islands
They scatter the bones of the pygmy mammoth
It is some remote substitute for blood they seek[a]
They are a nuisance of zipping mosquitoes.

They are on their exhuberant bombing runs
That is their work, a craft long disused
And they are under the gladsome,
Old-fashioned control of their pilots
Who, it is related, get very high and crazy
On the shocking hits of acceleration
And then return to the ground somewhere
Around suppertime, shout a lot,
And lift drinks to it in the officers' club.

---

a. They cannot be said to "fly" because they are projectile. And anyway, philosophically their overwhelming detroitness keeps them suppressed within the lower atmosphere.

Shifting an Interference with Nature to a Scientific Obstruction

Humming birds are close to junkies anyway
All that keeps them straight is the flower
And her control of plenitude in their cause
Curbing their overweening gluttony
And their insatiable singlemindedness
Yes, as the books say, they are pugnacious
But in them it is a quality absolutely without wit.

So when this normality is disturbed
And they go for sugar in water and acid red #27[a]
They do get vicious as the supply gets low.
At this point Harmonics drive these hovercrafters
Crazier still, as it punctuates their slavery[b]
And their birdbrained anger spreads
Throughout their frenzied holding patterns
Sugar, sugar.

---

a. Index number for the notorious red #2.
b. An experiment conducted at 110 degrees farenheit scale (a mere 70 degrees below the fundamental interval) by Jeremy Prynne, using the upper registers of a #365 Marine Band Hohner.

Del Mar

Del Mar was the favorite track of J. Edgar
And he used to take along his buddy, Clyde
One can see the golden mason ring glint wahoo
On the snowy Pullman napkin and african waiters
Serving ham and eggs, walkin with the car

They'd be put up in a mansion
Over by the water and their every wish
Taken care of with a catering snap.
Del Mar is a serious track: maybe too serious.

Wet Cake

Did you ever get the impression
standing in the supermercado
that an awful lot of people,
in California, want the *water*
but they'd just as soon skip the rain ?

What Will Be Historically Durable

About Nixon[a] there was
Something grandiose
Although this peevish society
Failed to even blink at it.

Nothing illustrates this
More than
When he stole the post office.

---

a. Yet, it is too easy to use one who's very name is a satire upon all government. (taken from Junius)

The Upwardly Mobile, and the Backs which Provide the Ladder

Isn't it ghastly
the way they've pilfered
from the workmanship.
They took the sprouts
right out of his mouth
and gave him a quick
rigidly compartmentalized dinner

They took his very pants
which was the *way* he dressed
and gave him something
with a little stretch to it.
Not that this was a service
especially after switching his dinner.

Chicken Relativity

Two thighs are better
than one
where one is better than none

An Opinion on a Matter of Public Safety

Air Bag sounds like eminent sickness
This device should not be permitted
General Motors was right to suppress it
and wrong to have relented
and Nader should stay out of it.

Driving is based on alertness
whether that be loose or tight
Those who let their attention wander
must not be encouraged to survive
by a bag full of air.[a]

---

a. Airbags are a good example of Say's Law, which says, that production creates, notoriously, the product, but the market also. And of course, the rationale, in this instance, Immortality.

Beyond the Air Bag

Sensing that Mediation is soon
to be carried too far, the majority[a]
are very queezy about being "read"
as *ready* for the neutron bomb.
The immediate floating of the idealogical Razor,
"kills people, saves property,"
creates a calculated tension between
what is human, and what is desired. Desire
is irrepressible.

---

a. Which includes everyone.

Beware the Plural of Usual

Oscar Wilde once expressed
the wish that poets should
have the same public access
as journalists, but that would
seem, in the present era, inappropriate
now the vastness
of their collusion has been revealed.

The superiority of the poem's report
always consisted in the power
to see through the veil.[a]

a. And therefore the least possible interference from information.

The Blue and the Green: Drugs and the Market

The division is so clearly now
among all things, the synthetic
and the grown. Taken together
they constitute the habit
of the whole population.

Yet human physiology is not up
to the current demand for extensions
which are everywhere strong, and
while not unprecedented, this is
the highest percentage ever seen of want.

And unnatural because the substances,
of alteration, were democratised
in the stimulus of the market.

When each glass of milk is a miniature suicide
The flowers of Oaxaca have a place on the shelf.[a]

---

a. The way the medical profession puts this is very flat.

To be good at sports
you must be spiteful
and horrible.

BILLY ELLEN TRAPP

You're Supposed to Move Your Head, Not Your Eyes

We now live next to the tennis court
Yellow green balls seem to be the thing
this season. For phrases we get
Vicious shot! Or, I *knew*
you were gonna do that!

Last Saturday we watched
the finals, inside. Vilas has got
an arm like a gorilla, and
it appears, it also serves
as his main instrument of thought
since it returns the ball
so often to the same place.[a]

Outside, on our court,
the less consecutive thocks and thucks
labor along on raw audible time
dramatized by the brain's impatience
with bleak, netted balls.

Connor's paranoid study of his strings
reminds the nation that tennis
is the only game in which the instrument
suffers the blame for error.[b]

---

a. A tennis intelligence is subtle up to but not including the shot.

b. Even the Dentist, that meanest class of sportsman, when he breaks your tooth, doesn't exclaim Shit! as he critically stares at his pliers. Footbol, both types, is perhaps least dialated by this instrumental paranoia. The passer does not glare in hatred at the hand which overthrew the pass, nor does the kicker inflict punishment on the foot that missed the goal. The hunter does not throw away the gun that missed the duck &c.

The Sociology of Games

In soccer
when you do something good
you get a hug and a kiss

In american football
when you do something good
you get a slap on the ass.

In Defense of Pure Poetry

The guards can say what they want
And so can Vernon and so can NBC
But whatever it is they have to say
Nobody can fault the King
For squeezing the trigger on Robert Goulet.

How Can One Not Blush to Accept Pay For Defending the Country

It is easy to see why
the voulnteer army doesn't work.
And it isn't that the salaries
are too low
to attract the citizenry.

The basis of mustering
should be property, to catagorize
those people who have
an interest in preserving
the state of their arrangements.

It is time the rulers of this country
revived that virtuous roman practise
of defending the state personally.

ALASKA: in Two Parts[a]

From the rear window of the Lockheed
we begin to pick out the Islands
of the green black archipelago
while inside the wingéd cocoon
a wild laughter issues from those
who go forth for the first time
cheered on by those who return again
to the expectation of this inflated emptiness.

This might feel like a certain moment
from the history of land grabs.
Another sublime promise
from a faithless future.
But the mode of transportation
changes everything except the mentality.
The desperation of walking
beside the household luggage
is lacking here, this is rather
a laughter of fraught nerves
not the undifferentiated search for space
we've always served.[b]
This is starting from thc shacks of Burkburnett
not from the salons of Kansas City.

---

a. For A. H., of Sitka.
b. There are two main kinds of cruelty: That which is enthusiastic, and that which is unnecessary. The period in which we live practises the latter.

The biggest single overcast
the longest white line
on the green tundra, the maginot
of this occulted place, like
a bumpersticker too famous to repeat.[c]
And the largest single cabbage
whose image is distributed on a post card
but as symbols, vegetables are dumb.

Across the gridline from The Voyager
stalwart stands the Captain Kook
"trusty" blondes in adamant short skirts
50¢ coffee, passable in extremis
1$ egg, a tradition from the Rush.
The food tastes like it was just
shipped in from Mars.[d]

Two men of equal height
appearing in pioneer beards
carry a vinyl couch[e] downtown.
Idling taxi outside window
speaks to a moose far out in the bush

---

c. The curious can ask around. I never once saw it on an actual bumper during several weeks of observation. There is a corrupted version of it in a photograph of a desk motto (sign) in N. Geog. #5, 150.

d. The domestics are said to eat wild meat from freezer coffins.

e. CH_2CH, a hydride derivative of ethylene, probably from Texas, probably from Gulf & Western, sure to cause cancer of the butt.

night falls, more gradual than slowmotion,[f]
this place is sultry
like a sunday school class.

The stories are thin and complicated[g]
destinations restricted.[h]
Brand new cars, hoodsprung, rimsprung.
Telephone dial tone an insect's buzz
an echo of the summer evening.
And then one day one wakes up sharp
with a great lump of ones in one's poke
a residue left over from the evaporation
of volatile fifty dollar bills.

II

We would have somewhat more interest
in reincarnation if there were
less insistence on mechanical joints
in the transmissions,
but it is perhaps too touched

---

f. The length and utility of summer day is notorious in latitudes near the Circle where the season becomes a diurnal extrusion and the sunne takes on the powerglides of a big Sandoz pill, and the population gets a little open-eyed rest in the brief crack of twilight. "The sky is full of parhelions of delusive glory."
g. Or ursine and certain, as an arm torn from its socket. The bears treat this place like muggers do Manhattan.
h. Big denomination dope and L.A. women might be the exceptions.

to dream of a return as a glacier
where that is a deeply turquoise dream,
a resonance of outside time.

Here we witness
the rumble of constant adjustment
here the earth moves, not
from the keenness of our perception
but from orogeny, its natural employment.

The blocking out and stringing
of the continent's shoulder
where the river is the mainline
and the island chain a broken arm
bent awry from the body.
A few natives will learn
to be its undertakers
among the horde of hikingboots[i]

Will this be, as it is publicised,
the last great land adventure?
Generally that's meant real estate.
We're not working with an exception
but for those who want the real thing
they're going to get it out of a can
or disappointment will rap their knuckles.
Trucking is not an adventure.
It's a service.

---

i. Athletic and æsthetic appreciation is invariably destructive. The force of nature is never considered destructive because its ends are unknown.

The creatures of ice feignt and advance
with a consciousness a great deal more
pervasive than the rise and fall of wages.
The tremendous pitch of their crystal stacks
the vast smell of their lunar coldness
the mammoth draft of their freezing humidity
the highminded groan of their polar turns.

From a beer-ad point of view
the fauna are impressive, evolved
to crush jeeps with a single swat,
and that's well enough, while socially
Alaska acts as the pardoner for every
haywire merchant with a will to get there.
But the power we behold is in the blue ice
and the delicate flora of the permenantum.
The people whose tradition it is
to live there will do best to carry on
picking up the threads of snow
from a system which is the book on survival.
That work will not be read
by all the cancritous Tej-okies
nor by the national geographic natives
in their copters & sanscrits.

Flywheel Programs

A Flywheel is a wheel with a heavy rim, and sometimes an unreciprocated counter, attached to a revolving shaft, in order to regulate motion, or accumulate power, for the same money. "The simplest form of work is the raising of a weight."

Distraction Control

The most oecological way
to kill the fleas
is to kill the dog.

Spuw Slang[a]

When I slam the door on your finger
I'm just milking your venom.

---

a. Spitting snake, *Norweg.*

Period Westerns

Insane how modern came late.
Just like the real world.
1937 ford sta. w., wood panels.
The glory of that era was wax.

Matchbook Covers I'll Probably Never Publish

Elizabeth Barret Browning
good nights make good mornings
Freddy Demuth
Montesquieu
isn't that pretty, Conway Twitty
Red Savine
Giddyup-go

On the Other Hand

In Emergency the pay is more
But of course in emergency
They run you to death

Light & Regularity

The beauty of the Inca month
is in its decimal clarity
three periods of 10 days each[a]

a. recorded along knotted strings, the "demonstration" for which we have only the metaphor—another example of our tendency to jump the sensational sequences of reality (tho of course we do have a reputation for jumping to maintain). The textural signals of fingertip perception are the preserve of the blind under optical dominance here, in which authority is so dispersed it is arbitrarily unavailable, hence the incessant lobby for local rule. Relative peace is balanced between the poles of Central Arrogance and Local Mercilessness. A lot of people are itching to take their pick, but of course Central Arrogance won't entirely let them. Some people say Thank God! Some say Dang it!.

On Stooping for Money

A waste of motion.
If you can hear it
When it hits the floor
It can't be worth much.

Category A Footnote[a]

Gibbon, speaking of the general
difficulties and irritations
both great and small, of Christians
living among pagans and their works:

> Even the reverses of the Greek
> & Roman coins were frequently
> of an Idolatrous nature. Here, indeed,
> the scruples of the Christian were
> suspended by a stronger passion.

---

a. #47, Chapt. XV, D. & F. of the R.E.

The Russian Quote

Oh poet, you should
get a Jobooski.

The Nature of the Phone

Don't forget
to pick up the milk, dear
and maybe we could use
another case of Olde Knothole.

Routine[a]

I'm Mrs. Fox,
I'm my husband!

a. In which the lady has rushed out of somewhere, probably the Kitchen, and is summoning what formerly was called Help, when such was on the market.

The Las Tycoon (A Review

There is something embedded
in the forgery
which is profounder
than the original
and which bypasses all
the original considerations.

Stuff the Voice-Print

Admission of error is a weakness
of judgement,
if one senses beforehand
that it will be seen
as a weakness.

Rauchenberg's Untitled (Early Egyptian Series

Some viewers might imagine
art is worth its weight. A work
which depicts that expectation
but which is essentially light
is Brilliant & worthless.

In Which We Are Paid the Dubious Political Compliment of Opposing Messages

During the week before May Day
I am handed a yellow bill
which tells me to normalize.
This is in plain view of a banner
spanning Grant street, China section
which urges me not to normalize.
I found myself wondering more & more
about arrangements with the Gang of 4.[a]

---

a. Because rationalism is invariably interesting.

Reapportionment of the Ceegar

The question is not
which came first
the chicken or the egg

The question is
which came last
journalism or tobacco

The Sanders Quote

Ye writes where ye can. With
your bloody finger on a prison wall
if necessary.

Claim Inspection

Mr. Kissinger was more
like Count Nesselrode
than that other guy.

A Tour of the Capital

Even if you didn't know a thing
you could read Chichén Itza.

A Thorobred Named Supreme Act

Listen, if anybody's saying,
you know, there's something new
and something or other's not
Well, they should look it up.

Sirius in January

It is swarming with planets
Time definitely repeats itself
That's its only job.

The Broughton Quote

My motto is:
attain the inevitable

A Short Study of Death

If you don't use your power you'll die.

Upping the Ante on Detente

Now we're hearing Stalin
wasn't good, he was *accurate.*

Among the Draperies of Definition

The Cobbett Quote

The learning is in the mind
not in the tongue: *learning*
consists of ideas *and not of*
the noise *that is made by*
the mouth.

Correct usages of some words widely misused or abused in modern conversation & poetry

VECTOR (S)

1. He (or she) smarted off until she (or he)
encountered a bullet of *flawless vector.* [Aero.]

2. A pile of steaming dogshit
covered with *buzzing vectors.* [Biol.]

3. He pulled a thick *wad of vectors*
from his pocket and peeled off 2 C-notes. [Econ.]

4. He stood with his legs apart, his dingo
pointed straight at Australia, both forelimbs
stuck deep in opposite sockets, his teeth
clamped down on a block of plywood, and
received a *lot of vector* parallel to his
axis, a summation extending throughout all
space. [Elec. Eng.]

CONDITION

1. The drinker sat on a simple chair
at a plain table, staring at the beer
whose *condition* was excited by a glow
discharge, operating at 10.6 microns
wavelength. [Brew.]

2. He took one look at the steaming pile of dogscat and said "Ye have *knavysche condycyouns.*" To which I replied, "Indeed, limits we did not set *condition* all we do." [Lit.]

HOG (S)

1. Yes, it is true, among all those sheep are not a few *hogs* [Vet.]

2. A hatless man (or woman) with a crewcut did *hog* the horse's mane. [Equest.]

JUXTAPOSITION (S)

1. Sure, there may be some interesting *juxtapositions*, but so what. [Anat.]

2. *Juxtaposition* is ok if you can't do anything else. [Sociol.]

ONGOING (S)

1. Farewell! my friends, I am *ongoing!* (as used by Liberian skippers). [Naut.]

2. The slavering from the patient-person's mouth went on for a fortnight

and there was obviously no end in sight. The disease was therefore described as *ongoing*, presumably because there was nothing *goingon*. [Catachr.]

LEFT WING URBAN GUERRILLAS

1. Ordinarily he would have made a *Left* turn but it was raining. And if there was one thing he never did, it was dip his *Wing* in the rain. Even for *Guerrillas.* He was just too *Urban.* [Crim. Psych.]

SUPPORTIVE (S)

1. A curate in the ancient town of Dursley, whose "habit" on entering a pub was to do a quick twirl so his cassock flew out like a girl's skirt and to throw his biretta over the bar so as to make a ringer on the sherry cask, on one occasion pulled his cassock up above his waist exclaiming "I'll show you how I keep cool." All he was wearing underneath was a tartan *supportive!* [Socio-Rel.]

2. "I would be more *supportive* were you less abortive." (overheard in a dark alley) [Milit.]

THROWEIGHT

1. I'm making a dogshit catapult
which I hope to market to people
who live on bluffs, or in flats
high above the city. I've taken out
a patent on a superb nickle-plated
guardrail mounting. I just haven't
worked out the *throweight* factors. [Diplo. Scat.]

GROSS NATIONAL PRODUCT

1. There's only one truly *Gross*
National Product, and that's . . . [Org. Chem.]

The Baron Macaulay Quote

(at that time) . . .
" . . . such an author as Fielding,
whose Pasquin had had a greater run
than any drama since the Beggar's Opera,
was sometimes glad to obtain,
by pawning his best coat,
the means of dining on tripe
at a cookshop under ground,
where he could wipe his hands,
after his greasy meal,
on the back of a Newfoundland dog."

An Unusual Accounting Treatment

We live in what is by definition
A slave society[a]
And this would include
most of the spread
We've always lived down the road
And have received or taken what we got.

Some of us have had a close practise
With the master
But whatever was gained there
would be only clearer
Certainly nothing more
And it will definitely be seen
By Kennecott's auditors
As of no consequence to the main facts.[b]

---

a. Relative freedom, illegal liberty.
b. It is too easy to see strictly industrialism in this model. Observational evidence indicates both these roles are loosely assigned and actively sought.

What Is This Thing Called Contemplation

Chewing an orbit
Considering a by-pass
Getting a transplant
Installing a plastic knee
Personally taking up
    more cubic space
    and reaping the satisfaction
    from Thereof
Considering a backpack *permanentum*
Rejecting a "backpack transplant"
    as too flamboyant
    and "too soon"[a]
    (tho, heaven knows, not
    too extravagant)

Thinking, however recombinant,
That jumping-the-gun, if
The gun were organic
And the jumping
Were suitably pure nylon
And the "the" were discarded
Like the pretentious rag it is
Could be interesting

And then, the inevitable
Note of caution: a dream a day,

---

a. Or too marsupial and too late.

A minolta,
A fast present, a blank past,
An immediate future,
A wait-and-see administration,
A non-religion,
A keep-moving rule
A no-credit ideal
A bad-debt result
An inch-a-minute public mind
    mounted on skids
An embarassed language
    in which Freedom
    is thrown like a shrunk bedspread
    over Liberty
    and "guilt" is the final,
    hard, unquestionable coinage,
    for which, of course,
    there is no registered mint
    and no busy signal.

Lending a Hand to the Inanimate

Rocks like to be skipped
It's the only occasion
on which they get to take off
and land.

1 0 1

One O one, that great Zero
Resting eternally between parallels

The 101 section was written one hand tied to the steering wheel, driving. I mention this not to demonstrate writing is still capable of illegality, but that it is necessary beyond considerations of place and time. A rather open scrawl while one's eyes are fixed to the road is the only trick to be mastered.

A View, From 101

One flew over the Cuckoo's nest
Playing right next to
Trailer Park Village

The factory neatly retailing
Its product

Easy, Oakland,
there's a roll-over
in the hotlane

Here and Now

The first hit of tobacum
the supreme rationality
exquisiteness as such

Try to extrapolate back
the pre-habit use
must have been to control
the Conference, the circle
glowing with power, the Pow-Wow
the resonance of mosaic.

Inspection

Poetry is now mostly government product
therefore we can dispense with the critical apparatus
the grades assigned to beef will do nicely:

Prime
Choice
Good
Commercial
Canners
Utility

Don't Get Your Hopes Up

1999 looks like they're
On The Job
Still drinking coffee
From styrafoam cups.

A Sense of Place

I'd live on the Moon
if the commute were
a little less.

People of Earth

You should check your calculations.
From a distance, it looks like
a chicken farm.

Man of Distinction

Only Barry
Manilow
will drive
you back
to eff emm.

An Unremote Recombinant

Eventually,
They're going to put you in a petri dish
And therein they're going to grow you.
Not all of you though. For instance
They're not going to grow your head
And they're not going to grow your body.

The Burr Quote

Law is anything which is
Boldly asserted
And plausibly maintained

2 Gulls Sittin On the Richmond Bridge

1st Gull says, looking at the freighter
off Angel Island, Which union
do you think the teachers should choose
to represent them?

Shit says Gull 2, Represent is a word
that won't bear much inspection.

Esperanto

There was a fair amount
of Ellis Island copy that summer.

It reminded me of the words
of Simon Bolivar:

The duty of every honest American
is to emmigrate.[a]

---

a. Quoted by G. Brotherston, *Latin American Poetry*, CUP, 1975.

Nebuchadnezzar's Dream,[a] A Variation for Dr. Christian Barnard

This great image,
whose brightness was excellent
stands before thee
and the form thereof is terrible

This image's head is of fine gold
his breast & his arms of silver
his heart a Baboon's
Belly & thighs of brass
Legs of iron
Feet of clay

---

a. The original of these verses from Daniel were taught me by David Southern.

The Gadsden Purchase[a] Revisited

We tend not to remember Gadsden
also negotiated the freedom of transit
for mails, merchandise and troops
across the Isthmus of Tehuantepec
when he bought that strip of Chihuahua.
A lighter and more sensible arrangement
than that fucking canal.

a. Used here to indicate grasp of idea rather than transaction.

If Somebody Asks You Where You Come From Remember

There are two catagories of soil
The soil of transport[a]
And the other is the soil of disintegration
Which can be found anywhere
but especially in mountains.
Runoff goeth down to the valley,
into the soil of transport.

---

a. And that would be anywhere between the Appalachians and the Rockies.

A Variation on Vallejo's #III

The layers are stilled by water
The waterhens are killed
And the entire general world fills
The night of the earth
Resting between glaciers, blocks,
Joints, the shoulder of the system
The stillness in the ice,
The grand specimens trapped there.

We are the children of weather maps
Our only book is a canyon
In twelve volumes, a work
Widely available in a shorter version.

Palms, Victory, Triumph, Excellence

My L.A. began in 1947
when I was in high school
and the derricks were still up.
I was fresh from Illinois
enlightened by Malinowski.

The excitment was not
in The Light, even then
beginning to be obscured
but in the Palm Trees
those companions
of the dinosaurs.

They are as snobbish as ethiopians
in their attitude toward man.
They follow him everywhere
except where it gets uncomfortable.

My favorite palms are in Riverside,
ol'downtown.
When someone told me
they are the preferred dwelling
of rats
I was emphatic in my disbelief
and in my disapproval of the possibility.

But of course, rats are smart.

Sunset

La Jolla is glittering this evening
They say we might get the green flash.

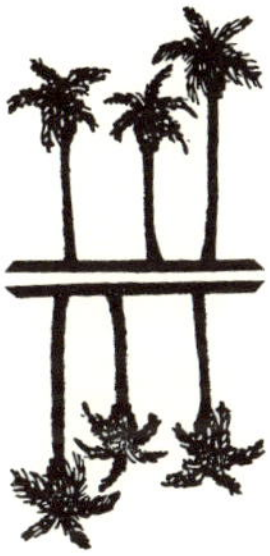

Printed June 1978 in Ann Arbor by Thomson Shore.
Typesetting and design by Graham Mackintosh, Santa Barbara.
The first edition consists of 3000 paperbound copies
300 trade clothbound copies and 100 copies signed and numbered
by the poet and bound in cloth by Cardoza-James, San Francisco.